Unsuspecting Cinderella

poems by

Shyla Shehan

Finishing Line Press
Georgetown, Kentucky

Unsuspecting Cinderella

*For Zoey and Cooper
who are the brightest stars
in the constellation of my life.*

*And for my husband Jim
whose love, support, and encouragement
never cease to amaze me.*

Copyright © 2022 by Shyla Shehan
ISBN 978-1-64662-806-3 First Edition
All rights reserved under International and Pan-American Copyright Conventions. No part of this book may be reproduced in any manner whatsoever without written permission from the publisher, except in the case of brief quotations embodied in critical articles and reviews.

ACKNOWLEDGMENTS

I am grateful to the editors of the following journals and publications where versions of these poems first appeared:

Gyroscope Review: "Trying to Read in the Castle Library"
HeartWood Literary Magazine: "Life and Death at the Castle"
Local Honey | Midwest: "To Whom or What or Where"
Sad Girl's Club Lit: "Pockets Full of Rocks"
The Showbear Family Circus: "Concourse B" and "Cure for the Common Equation"
Wingless Dreamer: "Semi-Charmed" under the title "Covid Sunset"
The Write Launch: "Castle Recursion" and "Castle Omnipresence"

I would also like to thank all the lovely humans who have supported me on my journey as a writer. In particular, I would like to thank the mentors who have read these poems and made them better with their care and attention: Jim Peterson, Teri Youmans, Graham Foust, Todd Robbinson, and especially Steve Langan who encouraged me to write the "Castle" poems.

Thank you to my children, Cooper and Zoey, for putting up with the hours I spend tucked away writing and endlessly revising. Thank you to Michelle Quick for her love of arts and crafts and for her friendship. And thanks, always, to my husband, Jim, for being my biggest fan and most attentive critic.

Publisher: Leah Huete de Maines
Editor: Christen Kincaid
Cover Art and Design: Michelle Quick
Author Photo: Jim Shehan
Interior Art: Zoey Punteney

Order online: www.finishinglinepress.com
also available on amazon.com

Author inquiries and mail orders:
Finishing Line Press
PO Box 1626
Georgetown, Kentucky 40324
USA

Table of Contents

Pockets Full of Rocks

    Still Life at Big Lake 1

    Pockets Full of Rocks 2

    Paper Shredder 3

    Hatchback Love 4

    Left Brain Poet 5

    When We Met 6

    Concourse B 7

    To Whom or What or Where 8

    Cure for the Common Equation 9

    Beginning at the Beginning Again and Again 10

And Then I Met the Castle

    The Castle that Swallowed My Castle 13

    Trying to Read in the Castle Library 16

    Masquerade at the Castle 17

    Abundances of the Castle 18

    Semi-Charmed 19

    Life and Death at the Castle 20

    Wandering Away from the Castle 21

    Brain Storming at the Castle 23

    Cake at the Castle 24

    Castle Recursion 25

    Castle Omnipresence 29

No Footnotes

    I Dream of Cheeseburgers 33

I. Pocket full of Rocks

Still Life at Big Lake

    We rode our bikes to a fat unripe pear. It was a Big Lake
we wandered around and found torn edges, yellowing and curved up
  at the corners. It was a half-moon pear sliced through with
pavement
              swallowed in cornflower blue flat wash when it rained.
      There was a playground dangling in the distance
    with busted swings on rusted chains. No children went there
or the ball field or the lake whose shallow pear bottom was a swamp
  with a "no swimming" sign sticking out. Rumor was,
    it was descended from a famous glacier,
            but you can't see that in the frame.
              There's just pale yellow loess rising around it,
    lined with trees twisting to a vanishing point.
Our grandfather was born and drowned there
        but we climbed out
                  and ran away.

Pockets Full of Rocks

Lying in my bed, I listened
to trains on tracks—their horns
blowing at reliable intervals.
Rhythm of the cicadas' persistent call
and rush of wind through tree branches
wheedled me into deep sleep
on many open-windowed
hot summer nights.
The world outside and I
had not yet been introduced.
I was only twelve or twenty then,

still turning in small circles
admiring the way my skirt wafted up.
I walked sidewalks around town
and trails in the woods discovering
what to collect.
Rocks were perfect
for slipping quickly into pockets
and were free, like time.

When I turned thirty-four
I was desperate for trains on tracks
and their nightly street-crossing calls.
I held the door for you.
I loved our inside jokes
about Bill and Ted and the fish lady
at our bank. I loved
all the ways you made me smile—

rocks stacked neatly in pots
against a far wall.

Paper Shredder

apathy enters unannounced stage left
demands a spotlight
a flipped switch
a mislabeled outlet
a mischievous three year old
a love letter
accompanied by an old photo
with no names on the back

strips of paper and rose flesh
scotch tape
hours hovering
recovering from hunching over
unrequited aching joints
unrewarded good deeds
unanswered calls
unsung
unwon
some things just aren't meant to be
undone

Hatchback Love

We found each other
in the back of your hatchback
on the side of some deserted county road.
A haze rolled in and cloaked the evening stars.
That night my body sank into yours
like sugar into melted butter.

We were an island in the mist,
a five year love affair,
perfection in the dark of night.
We were two souls intertwined
in a cliché—not meant to be.

Then the sun came out
and burned off all that
goddamned dewy-eyed newness.
We were lost.

Left Brain Poet

performs first successful memory transplant:
full report at ten.

I, for one, will search
for holes in the story, rearrange the scene—
burnt Sienna quietly snatched out
of a faded Nebraska sunset,
placed into Red Rocks around a stage in Colorado.
Substitution is not elevation for nostalgia
but protection from it.

I'm meeting myself for tea today
and can't decide if I'm ready—unsure
if I'm rehearsed enough.
I may never be.

When We Met

I wanted you to want me
like a fever breaking—
sweat pouring from every pore.
I wanted you to want my time—
a clock rewinding
to get more.
I wanted you to want my fingers
intertwined with yours—
footsteps side by side on sidewalks,
elevated spinning on dance floors.
I wanted you to want my words,
wade through my poetry
and ask after lines I cut.
I was hopeful—heart half open.
But you didn't and it shut.

Concourse B

I stare down a mirrored polished hall
from a seat at gate 25 in Concourse B—
space that harbors all the emptiness of blank paper.

My eyes close around a thought
as the mind rewinds.
There was a crack in the pavement

I tripped on once. The sidewalk goes on
and on and we walk
side by side or alone. There are cracks

we step on or over, on purpose.
Some we don't see until
it's too late.

I fondle faded memory
in the tensile tissues of my brain.
One moment tore me like a savage

and saturated my days—
hundreds of drenched pages,
journal entries, saved messages,

and unrecorded conversations.
My eyes open to forget.
The concourse is unchanged.

My paperweight glare mutes
quiet ramblings of families,
businessmen, and flight attendants.

I'm near the end of what I can sustain—
the sidewalk, the strain.
I leave my seat, my bag, the airport

and am never seen again.

To Whom or What or Where

It's been low tide
for a while, the beach
parched. Seagulls search
for salvation from starvation
and move on.

The sky is endless,
immeasurably clear.
I cast my questions out to sea
and marvel at the whole,
lonely Milky Way
from Here.

Cure for the Common Equation

I swallowed heaping teaspoons full
of forgets-where-it-has-been
and stacked bottles
of does-not-know-where-it-is-going
on the grey marbled kitchen counter
for tomorrow.

Neither were expected to have an affect
on my current condition.
which I was certain had no earthy cure.
Alas the mind is a well-oiled,
finely-tuned machine
designed to solve for X.

Solutions require removing variables.
Hence these two.
These too
are being removed
from realms of possibility—
down the throat and ruled out.
Stripped from the numerator
on both sides.

A cure for the common Y—
a cold sweat, broken heart,
loaded gun on stage, or
<insert anything here>
—can't be prescribed
or scribed before, or after.
Only during. Only now.

Beginning at the Beginning Again and Again

I keep trying to open my heart
but end up back here,
the place where all of us start.
In front of the bathroom mirror

I stare down at my crystal tumbler
and pluck his toothbrush from it.
Its bristles are still soft
and not yet curled.

Everything here has purpose.
A bin that holds travel-size soap
and shampoo. One for half-used chapsticks
another for cotton balls and Q-tips.

Not a thing among them
is a compass.

I look in the mirror
at the reflection of the toothbrush
in my hand
and can't even see myself.

II. And Then I Met the Castle

The Castle that Swallowed My Castle

I sacrificed so much
to be here.
I need you to know.

Once upon a time, I started over
with nothing.
Every dish and table acquired
was carefully selected—crafted
from my two hands and curated
from my brain. Pictures of my children
adorned walls and bookshelves
of my new home. Milestones
and insignificant moments
framed my story.
I spent years on their arrangement.

Ask me about the vase on the mantle
or the rock on my bathroom counter
from Colorado Springs.
In summer of 2009
Princess KK and her friend Lauren
from Oklahoma City
earned that space.

I had a painting in my living room—
a scene in Paris. People walking streets
near the Eiffel Tower—a remnant
of a former life. My grandmother admired it
and when she asked if she could have it,
I declined.

My home had two stories
and a finished basement.
The walls were ivory with windows
framed in oak. I was the house.

From the craft room in my basement
to the top of my witches hat,
it was me.

And then I met the Castle.
Now I'm moving
and all the moments
I've collected are being swallowed
whole. The digestion process
shreds my insides. My worry
where everything will go
is insatiable.

We need a room for crafting
and so we declare a room
that quickly becomes home
for everything
there is no other space for.
Plastic bins packed and stacked
to the ceiling—tables and chairs
piled past hope of ever crafting.

One room is eating three rooms
of my former home.
My office hugs the north wall.
My bedroom stretches out
while my daughter's bedroom hides
in the closet.
Plants that once drank
giant gulps of light
from a south-facing window
in a room above my garage
now get only small sips
of the setting sun
as it slides between the pines
that rise up from the backyard
of this new Castle.

We have a forest
of Christmas trees
in storage. How long
can my books survive in boxes
in the library?

There aren't walls
for my family—their "style"
doesn't really fit
with the Castle decor.
The children have space
enough for their present selves—
just not their past.

What is here is mine now
by proxy and proclamation
but I'm lost—living
in a Castle that's supposed to be us.

Trying to Read in the Castle Library

I sit in an overstuffed reclining chair in the library
surrounded on two sides by built-in shelves
populated with books that are not mine
with bookends and candles and odd trinkets.

There are windows on the other two walls
and a skylight overhead. The ceiling is sky blue
with clouds and a solitary bird—hovering.
My books are still in cardboard boxes.

I turn on every light
to trick my body into daybreaking—
to feign a place warm and lush
where unripe fruits find their way to sweet and red.

Instead my mind is heavy
with the dampness of the drapes,
lulled into contemplation by the rain's tap-tap
on the skylight, dark with overcast day.

The tapping turns into a code, turns into a message.
*This place will never be the lamp-lit blanket fort
your books were so sure was home.
Don't fight it, just go.*

I curl myself into a ball
and open umbrellas
on the inside.

Abundances of the Castle

There are indulgences that I'm not used to—
an over-full pantry, cupboards and closets
stacked with supplies, back-ups for back-ups,
enough for 100 rainy days.

Every need and whim accounted for—
last night I woke from a dream
and snuck away to write this.
There is a room just for that.

Ten rooms for entertaining guests.
No one hangs out in the soda fountain,
the sewing room or greenhouse—
the game room and bar kept clean for ghosts.

Life in the garden thrives—
even the weeds have their own bed.
I can now grow flowers
to fill every vase on every table in need.

Every *need* indeed.

Even a different steed in the stable
for each day of the week. It's absurd.
But I'm letting it all go, anyway.
What else can I do?

Masquerade at the Castle

I take two shots of vodka to drown the marching band
in my chest at the thought of the onslaught of people showing up
early or much too late to the castle. After guests arrive
I take two more shots—this time with cranberry for appearances.
I get into conversations I can't get out of and confess
the first time we had sex, it was in the greenhouse.

At nine, an unsolicited guest shows up without an invitation
and places a plate of cucumber sandwiches on the banquet table.
He strolls with authority across the lawn and later, unmasks me
on the balcony that overlooks the marbled swan fountain
and pond—asks me, *Where's the cocaine? I've seen pictures
of this place on Zillow.*

I don't stick around to see if he heads for the kitchens or back
to the party. I retreat to my sleeping quarters instead, exhausted
from vodka and visibility and exchanges with strangers. Lying
in my bed I hear one of the cats hacking after overeating again,
but I took a Xanax and am past having any part in caring.
It climbs on my back and starts licking my hair.

Semi-Charmed

Tonight the sky is alive with light—
golden rays spread wide as they reach
for flat cotton far in the distance.

I step out on the balcony and peer past
rows of perfectly spaced roofs—house
after house with people inside together

or alone. Light curtsies and blushes
at her dark lover's approach.
I watch their embrace and am swaddled

in insignificance.
I'm halfway home here. Always
halfway.

I stand with a full cup in wonder
of the chorus of colors and the sun
as it slides out of view.

Life and Death at the Castle

This place heals me
and wounds me.
I face west on castle grounds,
execute salutations to the sunset
stretching through up-dog and down.
Enchanting ivy grows lush
and wild over thresholds
and across archways. It climbs
the outside of the towers and creeps
into windows and door frames.
Finches build their own castle nest
inside the aviary. They lay eggs
and have offspring that can't survive—
voices lost in the middle of a song.
Three levels below, termites feast,
hollow the bones of this beast,
gather their numbers
and plan to ascend. This place
heals and wounds, though…

Won't it be fascinating to witness
the chew through?
Hounds released,
the topple of the towers,
ivy burned to its roots,
and the un-caged birds
set free.

Wandering Away from the Castle

I stand inside our bathroom closet
and face a pharmacy—
a plethora of little orange bottles
stare back at me.

Capsules and concoctions
for every pain and ache
to help when life refuses sleep
and cure fog when I wake.

And a special bottle of white pills
to help forget where I've been
when it happens (because it will)
that my heart breaks again.

I imagine escaping to the Oregon coast—
a life among trees beside the shore.
I'll curate a space for my books
and never want for more.

No horses in my stable there—
I'll walk to meet the Pacific tide.
I'll stand at my kitchen window
washing dishes with cats by my side.

My heart will swell in the garden
and I'll not need for a thing.
No collections or concoctions—
nor a heavy diamond ring.

I'll live on a hill in Lincoln City
with the Redwoods just due south
and waste time with some musician
who'll spirit poetry from my mouth.

Until then, I'll live in the castle
and daydream a life without pills
that promise to alleviate the aches
of all of my worldly ills.

Brain Storming at the Castle

I lay in bed and let thoughts roll around like cobblestones
or rocks on pavers. Or was it wind and hailstones
beating the paved ground? It was something
I was writing about that wanted to be more
but could not find the shape of itself.
What emerged was the story of a witch

    being ushered to the stake. Burning in fire
    was the trial that determined guilt.
    Words unfolded as the woman walked forward,
    unshackled and of her own accord.
    She lifted her hands, recited incantations
    that turned into miasma. Sound evaporated

        as she spoke, leaving a trail of acrid dust
        in the air. It floated down and settled
        on cobbled stones behind her. A throng
        of onlookers watched with wide eyes
        as she conjured doom. Damned the village—
        puritans and sinners alike—to drown

            under a field of ash. But I fell asleep
            before the volcano erupted out of the loess—
            its smoldering suspended. The language
            was wrong, the place and time and distance off—
            the point of view askew. This hailstorm story
            was not what I had wanted.

                The woman was a woman I wouldn't be
                until today.

Cake at the Castle

"Red flowers bursting down below us
    Those people didn't even know us."
        From the song, "I Bombed Korea"

Twenty-five years ago I didn't care much
about cake and have been lamenting
ever since how unimportant flavors are
and whether butter cream
or whipped cream
or cream cheese
would be a better base
for the best frosting you ever tasted.
Twenty-five years and I've still not mastered
how to politely say
I don't care about fucking cake.

Fuck your cake and eat it too
for all I care.

The only cake that I will serve at the castle
from now on is Sacramento style—
the kind that bombed Korea every night.

Yeah, that's the only kind of Cake
I've cared for
since I was nineteen.

If you come to the castle hungry
and decide to stay for dessert,
I might suggest
have pie.

Castle Recursion

On Tuesday
I wake early and fix breakfast
turn over the hourglass on the table
Out the door as chauffeur by 7:30
Personal trainer and nutritionist at 8:30
Errand maid at 9:30
Data Engineer from 10:30 to 3
I want to quit my job
Chauffeur again at 3
Taskmaster of homework from 4 to 5
not enough time to learn Spanish
Short order Chef at 5
Maid again at 6
Girlfriend from 7 to 9
not enough energy to learn
the language of love
dead to the world at 10
All the sand gone again

        *   *   *

On Wednesday
I sleep till ten
A friend stops by for lunch
We sip from full cups
of Bloody Mary mix and let our legs
dangle in the swimming pool
to the top of our calves
She asks if I do this every day
and I wonder why not
There is a stream behind us
lullaby sound of water
rushing over rocks
and a sweet breeze urges
go back to bed

He tells me I can quit my job
spend hours in the garden turning dirt
and tending to the vegetables
till my arms are stained yellow
past my elbows
pungent smell of tomato vine flesh
lingering on my fingertips for hours

      *   *   *

On Thursday
the sink is bottomless with dishes
Beds have unmade themselves again
Hungry fish in pond and stream bubble up
like a boiling pot
Cats with their fat naps
are awake and fighting again
Tile in the master bath is cracked
and the water refuses to drain

I spend four hours on the floor
exhausted by two in the afternoon
Cats are fighting again
I need to find the right tool
and screws for a project
Find three more projects instead
I need to quit my job

      *   *   *

On Friday afternoon
I walk the castle grounds
Iris and Lilies and Coreopsis Moonbeam
take turns worshiping the sun

My garden is a colossal mass
of climbing vegetables
As zinnias and marigolds are my witnesses
the tomato plants are now 7 feet tall
Soon the fruit will drag their branches
to the ground
Ripened red popping
amidst all that green
I don't want to miss a minute of this
I'll probably quit my job

In the evening the Castle master comes home
from business and our words collide
in a rush of news from the day
A Venn diagram that intersects
at cats and children and our future
We're planning an outing and a party
We're scheming about tomorrow
We're falling asleep
in the middle of sentences

    * * *

On Sunday
we sleep past 8
Wake with eager arms and hands
Linger huddled in conversations
and much-needed affection

We have breakfast until noon
Venture out into the world
on one of our many steeds
in search of treasure

    * * *

On Monday
I conspire with the prince and the princess
Comforted by having someone
to talk to about a plan
I begin again in the kitchen
and check the grocery list
before I leave for the market
I re-organize the pantry
and check our schedule for appointments
Stand at the sink and worry
I'm not pulling my weight here
Perhaps I should get a job

This afternoon I lie down
in the greenhouse with the cats
and listen to Arcade Fire again
Among the rocks
stacked neatly in pots
against a far wall
is an orchid in bloom.

Castle Omnipresence

This place is not necessarily haunted; it is inhabited by a force.
A dark chill loiters in the vacant basement
conversing with the termites who are otherwise occupied
with their colony plans. Dense fog hangs in the garden
when the rest of the houses on the block are lit up by sun.
Small creatures scurry with frantic claws that scrape wood
inside the ceiling above the master bed. I pull the blankets tighter
and wait for larger predatory claws that follow.
Strange artifacts have been placed carefully throughout the house.
When asked, the current owner explains they were there
when he moved in. Yet, new antiques appear almost weekly.
The force feels ever-present—observing
but never interfering in our daily lives. It reminds me
of something I heard about God—supernatural
and subject to mood swings and unnatural occurrences.
I wonder if I should offer gifts
or learn how to pray.

III. No Footnotes

I Dream of Cheeseburgers

fat and juicy
smothered in cheddar cheese
shoestring onions on a toasted brioche bun
maybe with barbeque sauce this time
please
don't hold the fries

maybe I'm just hungry because I'm starving myself
to fit into a heavy white dress
not white though—ivory
you only get one shot at white
and that was wasted
because I was already wasted at 19

already rehearsing lines off white pages
a script handed to me
before I could read
I, a toddling tot with my baton
in a royal purple sequin leotard
and twirling skirt

on my wedding day I wore earrings
that belonged to my paternal great-grandmother—
tiny white pearls in a dainty gold setting
something old
an exact quote from page 22
everyone looked so pleased

I followed nearly all the instructions
yet I failed and was left
alone
with hundreds of lines
and no footnotes
on how to begin again

Shyla Shehan is an analytical Virgo who was born in Iowa and has spent the majority of her life in the Midwest. She holds an MFA in Writing from the University of Nebraska where she was awarded an American Academy of Poets Prize. During her time in the program, she leveled up her poetry game and discovered that writing has more to offer than just a way to cope with the chaos of the Universe.

Her work has appeared in *The Decadent Review, High Shelf Press, Ocotillo Review, Plainsongs, Gyroscope Review,* and elsewhere. Her most noteworthy accomplishment to date is divorcing her (now former) career as a Healthcare IT Integration Specialist. Since then, she has pledged her undying love and fealty to Poetry but has so far refused to get matching tattoos.

Shyla is co-founder and editor of *The Good Life Review* and lives in Omaha, Nebraska with her husband, children, and four cats. She is currently suffering a mini-midlife identity crisis over writing this bio but is nonetheless grateful to you for reading and hopes you will visit shylashehan.com for more.

www.ingramcontent.com/pod-product-compliance
Lightning Source LLC
LaVergne TN
LVHW041558070426
835507LV00011B/1173